FINDING THE YES IN THE NO

A Guide to Overcoming Rejection

PAULA SON-CALDWELL

FINDING THE YES IN THE NO

Unless otherwise indicated, scripture quotations are taken from the King James Version of the Bible. Copyright © 1979, 1980, 1982 by Thomas Nelson, Inc. All rights reserved. All definitions taken from dictionary.com.

All Rights Reserved. No part of this book may be reproduced or transmitted in any form or any manner, electronic of mechanical, including photocopying, recording or by any information storage and retrieval system, without permission in writing from the author/publisher.

Copyright © 2014. Paula S. Caldwell

All rights reserved.

ISBN: 978-1-312-32464-0

PAULA SON-CALDWELL

TABLE OF CONTENTS

Endorsement..5
Dedication..6

PART 1: THE FOUNDATION

1	THE DICHOTOMY OF REJECTION	9
2	FINDING THE YES IN THE NO	15

PART 2: SATAN'S METHODICAL USE OF REJECTION

3	SYSTEM IS UP AND RUNNING	37
4	IDENTITY THEFT	48
5	PUZZLE PIECES: FUNCTIONAL DYSFUNCTION	53

PART 3: DEALING WITH REJECTION

6	THE TRUTH, THE WOUND, THE SCAR	61
7	OUT OF CONTROL	68
8	THE SILENT KILLER	76
9	DEAL WITH IT	81

PART 4: OVERCOMING REJECTION

10	GET THE ROOT OUT	89
11	FROM "WHY NOT" TO "WHAT NOW"	94
12	DO SOMETHING DIFFERENT	100

PART 5: DISCOVERING GOD'S PURPOSE THROUGH REJECTION

13	AN INSIDE JOB	107
14	PRESERVED ON PURPOSE	112
15	IT'S ALL ABOUT YOU	116

Acknowledgements......................................123

ENDORSEMENTS

Finding the Yes in the No is revolutionary! On planet earth, who has been spared the challenge of rejection? NO ONE! With Paula's easy-to-read, concrete steps and biblically based summary, EVERYONE can receive relief and encouragement 'to let God DEVELOP the "you" He needs for His Kingdom.

A life altering read. Thank you, Paula.

Kathy K. Charley, M.A.
Licensed Clinical Christian Counselor
President, Personal Growth Association
Certified Academic Institution of the National Christian Counselors Association

DEDICATION

This book is dedicated to Sandra Hawkins Guice. Because of your simple question and my inability to find an appropriate answer for you at the time, I was prompted to write this book to hopefully give you an answer. I pray you always find a YES in the NO!

This book will help you realize that life does not stop at NO! There is still a YES and an opportunity to make progress!

~PSC

Journal entry on October 19, 2011

On this morning as I was driving to pick up Alex from work, the most amazing thing happened. I wasn't speeding and I noticed ALL of the lights were green! Even as I turned from the one-way street onto another street, green lights! I remember seeing lights being green from a distance and thinking, "There's no way these lights will remain green by the time I approach them." I didn't speed up, but I kept cruising and obeying the speed limit regulations. I said to myself, "If I make it through this last light, I'm going to scream!" Well I made it through the last light and I began to scream and then God gave me a revelation.

The revelation was: "When it's your season, NOTHING will hold you back. The path will be clear. Even when you see things ahead of you that would potentially stop you, when you get to it, you will be able to go through it! The thing that will hold someone else up and impede progress will not apply to you. You will be able to go through it with ease!" *Because I have the "green light," I can find the YES in the NO! ~PSC*

PART 1

THE FOUNDATION

1
The Dichotomy of Rejection

When looking at rejection from the perspective of how Satan uses it and how God uses it, one can easily conclude that the purpose for the rejection is isolation; however, the purpose for the isolation is totally different. If God & Satan use rejection for isolation, then it is imperative to get clarity of the dual purpose. Satan's ultimate purpose for using rejection is to get you to isolation to destroy you; whereas, God's ultimate purpose for using rejection to get you to isolation is to develop you! God can use the isolation to destroy the "you" He does not need. He can also use the isolation to develop the "you" He needs that will make a great impact for His kingdom! How can the enemy destroy you with isolation and God develop you with isolation?

Let's ponder this idea: The enemy will use rejection to get you all alone; and begin to tell you everything that is contrary to what God has said concerning your life. Everything Satan does is strategic and sometimes these things happen when you least expect it. Who expects Satan to come after them after a mountain top experience? I believe the Bible gives us clarity as to when to expect an encounter with Satan. I would even be bold enough to say sometimes he doesn't say things to you contrary to what God has told you; but He camouflages the Word so that you can't really decipher the truth.

Referring back to the timing of the enemy, let's look at how he tried to mislead Jesus right after he finished fasting in Matthew 4: 1&2:

"Then was Jesus led up of the spirit into the wilderness to be tempted of the devil. And when he had fasted forty days and forty nights, he was afterward an hungered."

Satan appeared during Jesus' isolation to ultimately destroy him; and He tried to destroy him with the Word of God. It can be implied that Satan will not try to destroy you with what you don't know. That would be too easy and you would be aware of his devices. On the contrary, Satan comes to destroy you with what you know, with what is closest to your heart and with what is on your mind.

FINDING THE YES IN THE NO

God will allow rejection to get you to a place of isolation to develop you. I want to reiterate that He will use the isolation from the rejection to destroy the "you" He does not need and to develop the "you" He needs for His kingdom. If we look at the same Scripture in Matthew 4: 3-10, we see the isolation, but we also see how God develops Jesus in the Word. Satan continued to approach Jesus by using what was closest to Him, but because Jesus was aware of who he was, He was able to defeat him.

I propose to you to become familiar with who your enemy is and when he tries to use those things closest to your heart and mind, you can use the power that God has given you to rebuke him. When you begin to read the Word of God and study it, you will be able to rebuke Satan by simply saying what God's Word says about you and about your situation. Remember God is trying to develop the "you" He needs for His kingdom.

If you refer to Acts 9, that story of the conversion of Saul to Paul is an appropriate example of how God will isolate you to destroy the "you" He does not need and develop the "you" that is needed in His kingdom. He has to destroy the "you" that is not useful in your purpose. The "you" that gets easily offended, the "you" that responds in a way that is contrary to what you say you believe, the "you" that wants to curse people, the "you" that wants to defend yourself, the "you" that responds out of emotions, the "you" that lacks maturity for your purpose.

Pray this prayer:

Lord I thank you for opening my eyes to see how isolation serves as a purpose in rejection. Lord I pray that you help me to continue to see and understand this process through the spirit. I pray that you keep my mind and my heart during times of isolation when it can be difficult. I pray that you gently remind me in times of doubt how the isolation is working for my good. Lord I pray that you continue to take out of me what does not reflect you during the times of isolation. Thank you for caring enough for me to work on me in private so that I can be an open display of your glory and favor. I thank you for hearing and for answering my prayer. In Jesus, name, Amen

2
FINDING THE YES IN THE NO

At some point in our lives, all of us have dealt with or will have to deal with rejection; be it as a child, teenager or adult. We deal with rejection in every developmental stage of our lives. Rejection itself can be harsh because at first it seems as if it is the final answer. According to Dictionary.com,

REJECT means: *To refuse to have, take, recognize, etc.; to refuse to grant (a request, demand, etc.); to refuse to accept (someone or something); to discard as useless or unsatisfactory; to cast out or off or eject.*

FINDING THE YES IN THE NO

In short, rejection in its simplest form is the word NO, and who likes to hear "NO"?

The scenario goes something like this: You ask for something or apply for something. In your mind the likelihood of receiving or obtaining your desire is great; but, for whatever reason, it is not granted to you. You feel rejected because you have been refused something that you desire. If you allow those instances to take root in you, you begin to think from the mindset of rejection.

We all have experienced rejection in our lives in various forms. For example, you want to be friends with someone and that person doesn't want to be your friend, or, when a parent compares their children to their siblings or other children early on that child begins to feel as though he/she is not "good enough". Perhaps as a teenager you were trying to fit in with certain peer groups, or wanted to participate in organized sports and you didn't "make the team"; maybe you weren't accepted into the college you applied for; or perhaps, you weren't accepted by the sorority or fraternity you initially desired. And ultimately, the big one that we all have experienced, for some more than once, was being rejected by someone you wanted to date and that person did not feel the same way about you. Rejection is not only reserved for youth, but as an adult, being denied a certain job, being denied a promotion, being denied the car you wanted or the house you wanted. All of these on varying levels are forms of rejection.

The word NO is equivalent to rejection. One of the most difficult things to comprehend is to know you're adequately qualified for the thing or things you are going after and yet you still hear "NO".

FINDING THE YES IN THE NO

Let's examine what happens in that moment immediately following the rejection. How do you feel? There is probably an instant sorrow, which is accompanied with a feeling of hopelessness and helplessness. There is also a sadness that immediately happens that generally cannot be remedied easily with the common phrase, *"Everything will be alright."* Tears may begin to fall, tears of pain and lack of understanding. Sometimes you may even feel as though you can't go any further because you feel you have exhausted all of your options. What is your next move if you feel this was your last resort and you still got rejected?

This is the perfect time to find the YES in the NO!

In order to find the YES in the NO there must be certain qualities you possess as an individual. You can ask yourself questions like:

- o Am I patient?
- o Do I possess perseverance?
- o Am I certain of my purpose in life?
- o Am I optimistic?
- o Am I open to correction?
- o Do I let my emotions control my decisions?

Based on the way you respond to these questions, it can be determined if you have what it takes to find the YES in the NO. Let's examine these questions and how they pertain to finding the YES in the NO.

FINDING THE YES IN THE NO

AM I PATIENT?

In order to find the YES in the NO you must have patience. PATIENCE is: *An ability or willingness to suppress restlessness or annoyance when confronted with delay; it is the quality of being patient, as the bearing of provocation, annoyance, misfortune, or pain, without complaint, loss of temper, irritation, or the like.*

To find the YES in the NO you must possess a willingness to suppress restlessness when confronted with delay. So then what is the delay? The delay is NO!

Have you ever noticed while driving on a road or highway that is under construction, there may be a black sign with amber letters that says **EXPECT DELAYS**? With that sign, the Department of Transportation has warned you, just in case you are late or running behind, that there is a possibility that because of road work your journey may be delayed. Not only should you expect it, but, you have to make adjustments or accommodations for it.

What if God warned you just as the DOT has those black signs with the amber colored electronic letters that says "EXPECT DELAYS?" How would you handle it? I believe that sign triggers something in you to have patience. It prepares you for what might happen because they are under construction and trying to make accommodations for everyone, not just for the workers who are working on the area, but also for the people who are traveling on the roads. So what if in that NO, in that delay, God is making sure everyone has the appropriate accommodations for the situation? He's not just focusing on you, not just the person you are becoming, but also for those coming after you and those who have to interact

FINDING THE YES IN THE NO

with you! If you are going to be able to find the YES in the NO, you must have **patience**.

Pray this simple prayer: *Lord I pray for the patience I need when I am faced with a NO in a particular situation. Give me the patience I need in order to see the delay in the situation as a good thing. Grant me the patience to wait in the middle of an uncertain circumstance. Help me to stand and not give up in the face of delay; but to make the appropriate adjustments in my thinking that will allow me to understand that I am still in your will; even in the face of NO. Lord I believe you are making me so that I can accommodate what is on the other side of the delay. Not only are you making me to accommodate it, but you are making it to accommodate me. Lord I thank you for hearing and for answering my prayers. In Jesus' name, Amen*

DO I POSSESS PERSEVERANCE?

Another trait you must possess in order to find the YES in the NO is **perseverance.** Patience and perseverance are similar, but there is a tiny difference. **PERSEVERANCE** is: *A steady persistence in a course of action, a purpose, a state, etc., especially in spite of difficulties, obstacles or discouragement.*

You have to be persistent in spite of difficulties (NO), obstacles (NO) or discouragement (NO). You must be persistent in knowing that there is still a YES in the middle of this and you must be patient enough to see whatever the delay is through. You must develop a thought pattern of knowing if it didn't happen, it's because it's just not time; either you're not ready for it or it is not ready for you. You must stay on your course of action and remember your purpose regardless of the NO.

In spite of the NO, you have to keep moving forward even if you have to pause, regroup and rethink your strategy. The human mind must remember what God says in Isaiah 55:8,9:

"For my thoughts are not your thoughts, neither are your ways my ways, saith the Lord. For as the heavens are higher than the earth, so are my ways higher than your ways, and my thoughts than your thoughts."

We may think we have so many things figured out in reference to how God does things, but we must understand the huge gap between the heaven and the earth. That's how far our thoughts, plans and ideas are from God. There is not a numerical measurement that can accurately determine the distance between heaven and earth. Therefore there is a lot of room for error in our thoughts and assumptions when we consider the gap between heaven and earth.

Pray this prayer: **Lord I ask that you equip me with the perseverance I need in the face of this obstacle, in the face of this NO. Give me increased perseverance to see the YES in the NO. Help me to stay the course according to what you have spoken concerning my life. I acknowledge I have tried to figure things out and sometimes tried to work things out on my own. I realize when I try to figure things out and work things out my actions suggest that I put you out. Lord help me to submit my ways and my thoughts to you. I realize there is a gap in the distance between heaven and earth and my thoughts and my ways generally are extremely different from yours. I ask that you forgive me for my error and help** *me to do better. Lord I thank you for hearing and for answering my prayers. In Jesus' name, Amen*

AM I CERTAIN OF MY PURPOSE IN LIFE?

In order to find the YES in the NO, you must have a clear understanding of God's purpose for your life. You must know that if God didn't allow it, it is still working towards His purpose for your life. If you received a **NO**, you have to rest assured that it is a **YES** as it lines up with your purpose. If there is any doubt in what God has purposed for you to be, then there will be a heightened level of uncertainty and confusion in the face of rejection. Not saying there won't be uncertainty even if you do know your purpose, but it is easier to accept and totally trust in a God who knows everything; including the steps you must take to fulfill your purpose. Commit to knowing and being assured of your purpose, and that way you can see the YES in the NO.

Pray this prayer: **Lord I thank you right now for where I am and where you have led me to up until this point in my life. Where this is uncertainty as it relates to my purpose, I pray that you give me clarity. I know with clarity will come an increased acceptance to everything that is in line with your will, even if it includes a NO every now and then. I ask that you forgive me for any time I have wasted being unsure as it relates to my purpose. Lord I thank you for hearing and for answering my prayers. In Jesus' name, Amen**

FINDING THE YES IN THE NO

AM I OPTIMISTIC?

Another characteristic you must possess in order to find the YES in the NO is the ability to be optimistic. I would dare to say that is one of the most important traits.

OPTIMISM is:

1. *A disposition or tendency to look on the more favorable side of events or conditions and to expect the most favorable outcome.*
2. *The belief that goodness pervades reality.*

I'm sure you have heard the question: How do you see this glass of water? Is it half-empty or half-full? An optimistic person would reply with seeing it as half-full. That person will find the positive in any situation and expect a favorable outcome. This person will find a favorable outcome even in the face of a NO. An optimistic person will have these possible responses when given a NO:

- NO means not now or not yet
- NO means there is something better
- NO is not the final answer
- There is life after the NO
- NO is a way of redirection
- NO is just an opportunity to seek God more and stay in His face
- NO is God's way of preventing me from something that is potentially life threatening

NO is God's protection!

Pray this prayer: **Lord I thank you for the NO's I have encountered in my life. I pray that you help me to see the good in any type of rejection I may face. I pray that you give me the grace to understand that your**

NO is still a YES because it is working towards your ultimate plan and purpose for my life. Your NO is still a YES because it is working for my good. Lord I ask that you forgive me if I viewed a NO as the end of the world, and not the beginning of a different direction. Lord I thank you for hearing and for answering my prayers. In Jesus' name, Amen

AM I OPEN TO CORRECTION?

As human beings, there will be times when we don't get things correct. There will be times either through error in our thinking, or some maladaptive form of thinking we have acquired, when we will simply be wrong! Let's look at what the Bible says about correction or chastisement in Hebrews 12:6-11:

"For whom the Lord loveth he chasteneth, and scourgeth every son whom he receiveth. If ye endure chastening, God dealeth with you as with sons; for what son is he whom the father chasteneth not? But if ye be without chastisement, whereof all are partakers, then are ye bastards, and not sons. Furthermore we have had fathers of our flesh which corrected us, and we gave them reverence: shall we not much rather be in subjection unto the Father of spirits, and live? For they verily for a few days chastened us after their own pleasure; but he for our profit, that we might be partakers of his holiness. Now no chastening for the present seemeth to be joyous, but grievous; nevertheless afterward it yieldeth the peaceable fruit of righteousness unto them which are exercised thereby."

In order to find the YES in the NO, you must be able to be corrected. The NO is still the YES if you look at it through the eyes of correction. If you understand your Father knows what you need and what you do not need, He knows the correction you can endure. Even the Bible says in the moment of correction, it is not pleasant, but afterwards it will yield the fruit of righteousness. You have got to understand that a NO is temporary, not eternal.

Pray this prayer: **Lord I thank you for loving me enough to call me your child. I understand the correction you give me is because you love me and your ultimate desire is to have me walk in the purpose you have created for me. I admit sometimes I don't like the way you correct me and I may even act like a spoiled brat. Forgive me for not seeing your correction as a good thing in my life. Forgive me for always wanting things to be my way and not being able to see things as you see it. Forgive me for trying to fix** *things even when it is not meant to be fixed by my interference.* Help me to be a better person, a more mature child of yours so that I may endure correction and understand the NO you are giving me is only temporary. Lord I thank you for hearing and for answering my prayer. In Jesus name, Amen!

DO I LET MY EMOTIONS CONTROL MY DECISIONS?

We are familiar with this popular quote: **"*Don't make a permanent decision based off a temporary circumstance.*"** Many of us have been and are guilty of doing this very thing because we respond to things from our emotions and not from a sound mind. Have you ever done something you regretted? Have you ever said or done something in the heat of an argument, but after things cooled down you regretted it? That's a prime example of making a permanent decision based off a temporary circumstance or inconvenience. Yes, it does require you to have the ability to exercise self-control in these situations, and not only self-control, but if you are known for "flying off the handle", I would even suggest you add an accountability partner or two who can help you consider future repercussions. You need people who can help you to think about how your actions in the moment can't be erased and how "I'm sorry" doesn't clean things up.

In order to find the YES in the NO, you have to get past your initial emotional response when you hear the word NO. It is possible that the NO can be temporary, but your actions can make it permanent.

Pray this prayer: **Lord I thank you for how you have created me and everything that makes me who I am in you. Lord I admit there are times I respond based off my emotions and those are usually responses I wish I could take back. I acknowledge the faults in my decision-making based on the poor results or lack thereof because of the place in which I made my decisions. I resign my right to have an emotional response. I resign my right to react to my "hurt feelings" because I did not get the YES I was expecting. I ask that you forgive me for messing things up and pushing things further back when I could have just submitted even my out of control emotions to you. I ask that you help me to do better and help me to control myself in the heat of the moment. Lord I thank you for hearing and for answering my prayer. In Jesus' name, Amen**

PART 2

Satan's Methodical Use of Rejection

3
System is Up and Running

Have you ever been a victim of a theft? Whether someone forced his way into your home or your vehicle; or someone stole your wallet or purse; perhaps someone violated you by stealing your innocence, etc. The list could go on. But the goal here is to get you to revisit the feelings you experience when you realized something was taken from you.

There is a scripture in the Bible that gives a clear reference to the purpose of Satan. The Bible states in St. John 10:10a (KJV): *"The thief cometh not, but for to steal, and to kill, and to destroy"*

FINDING THE YES IN THE NO

When you look carefully at this Scripture, you can see how Satan is systematic in his mission. Although his plan is to ultimately destroy you, he starts by weakening. Blow-by-blow, the enemy takes jabs at your strengthened stature. In his method of stealing, he targets trust and comfort. In killing he aims for the heart and relationships. In destroying, he deals with the mind and ultimately your life. In short, the enemy wants to weaken you so that he has access to eventually destroy you.

Rejection has a way of impacting a person psychologically and then emotionally.

Rejection opens the door for the enemy to come in because it creates vulnerability in the mind and the emotions, which coincides with the enemy's strategy of stealing. When something is stolen, it can be implied that there was an entry that gave the culprit access to the desired target; be it known or unknown to the victim. The perpetrator finds a weak space to gain access or a space that will allow for forced entry. Often times it is not something that is obviously seen to the unsuspecting victim; but the offender puts in time to study the easiest way to conquer.

Let's take a closer look at how the enemy uses rejection to steal something from you or to weaken you. When rejection impacts a person psychologically, the person begins to live a life from the mindset of defeat, stagnation and fear. Rejection does something to the brain, which brings on a cautious approach. It does something in the emotions, which impacts the self-esteem of the individual because it makes a person have thoughts of "I am not good enough." If one is not careful, rejection will keep a person from moving forward. The enemy will use rejection to keep a person bound and stagnant. As a matter of fact, if allowed, it will alter the way a person makes decisions for the rest of his/her life.

Pray this prayer: **Lord I come to you today as the Creator of all things, Creator of my mind and my emotions. Lord I admit that I have experienced some rejection and I recognize how it has impacted me psychologically and emotionally. I recognize the places of fear and places of stagnation in my mind and emotions. Lord I pray that you release me from these strong holds in my mind and emotions. I pray that you give me the mind which was also in Christ Jesus when He experienced various forms of rejection. I expect to see a difference in my thinking and in my emotions because you now have control. I will apply Philippians 4:8 to my life from this day forward. I** *thank you for hearing and answering my prayer. In Jesus' name, Amen*

<u>Rejection will weaken your ability to make sound/rational decisions!</u>

Because a plan in the enemy's systematic scheme is to weaken you so that he has access, he uses rejection to undermine your ability to think and make sound/rational decisions. He wants to weaken your belief in your God-ordained purpose and weaken your trust in the God you say you serve. His goal is to have you to rely on your own ability and strength and to cause you to make decisions without seeking God. He desires to have you thinking and operating from a place of hurt and bitterness. He longs to have you blind to your ultimate purpose so that you may live an unfulfilled life, accomplishing nothing. His goal is simply to keep you bound. He wants you to be bound by the results of the bad decisions you made as a result of the rejection you experienced.

Pray this prayer: **Lord I come to you because I admit I have relied on my own ability to make decisions. Not only have I relied on my own ability, but also my decisions have been made from a weak place; a place of rejection. Lord I ask that you forgive me right now for not submitting totally to you in my decision-making. I ask that you forgive me for being my own personal god. I pray that you grant me the grace of another chance. I do see how my decisions have not been beneficial and how they have gotten me off track. I pray that you give me clarity of mind as I try to live out each day. I pray that you restore my sound mind to make good decisions. I pray that you fortify my mind in you so that I am no longer weakened by the rejection that I experience. I submit** *to your word in Proverbs 3:6 and I will acknowledge you in all of my ways and let you direct my path. I thank you for hearing and answering my prayer. In Jesus' name, Amen.*

<u>Rejection will cause you to settle for something/ someone God never intended for your life.</u>

Pray this prayer: **Lord** *I come to you right now asking you to forgive me. I ask for forgiveness because I know I have settled and allowed things and people into my life that you never intended for my life. I admit this settling was a result of the way I felt after I experienced rejection. I recognize my fault and I acknowledge that I have tried to fix the situation according to what I thought I needed in my life. I acknowledge that in my limited thinking and damaged* *emotions, I made some decisions that have not been good for my life. Lord I realize you allowed me to live with my decisions, but I thank you for opening my eyes to a better way. I realize it may be a little difficult to release those things I have granted access into my life; but I do know you have the power to help me move forward with no attachments. Lord I pray that you sever every attachment that I have settled for as a result of rejection and give me the strength to accept your will for my life. I thank you for hearing and answering my prayer. In Jesus' name, Amen*

<u>*Rejection will cause you to try and fix things on your own!*</u>

Pray this prayer: **Lord I ask that you forgive me** *for trying to do your job. Forgive me for stepping in the way to make something work that you did not* *intend to work. Forgive me for being so eager but yet so naïve in wanting something you did not want in my life. Help me to see beyond what I see right now and understand your will for my life. Help me to take my hands off things that will not work no matter how much I try to fix it. Help me to resolve to trust you when I want to trust myself. Help me to let go of my right to do what I think will work. I believe you know what's best for me and I trust in your sovereignty. Thank you for hearing and answering my prayer. In Jesus' name, Amen*

<u>Rejection will cause you to waste time and energy!</u>

Pray this prayer: **Lord** *I am sorry for not being a good steward of my time and my energy by using it on something or someone you are not allowing in my life.*

FINDING THE YES IN THE NO

I am sorry for wasting time on something that will not yield a return in my life. I'm sorry I did not get it the first time when it didn't work. I realize I have lost time being happy and being productive because I chose to try to invest time and energy on a dead end situation. Lord I pray that you redeem my time. Give me back the time and energy I lost. I commit to doing better and understanding I cannot fix what you do not want to work. Lord I thank you for the grace you have given me to get through this situation. I thank you for opening my eyes to what was a seemingly dead-end situation. I thank you for hearing and for answering my prayer. In Jesus' name, Amen

Rejection creates vulnerability in a person and it dilutes the authenticity of the truth!

Pray this prayer: **Lord I come to you in a vulnerable state. I admit I am vulnerable because of the impact of rejection in my life. My vulnerability has weakened my ability to decipher the truth of any situation. I acknowledge that I have given the enemy access to my mind and my emotions and things have become blurry to me. I admit I have a problem seeing and accepting the truth. Lord I give to you my vulnerable place and ask that you fill it with strength, wisdom and insight. I ask that you remove everything the enemy has placed in me such as doubt and suspicion and replace it with trust and assurance in you to recognize the truth of any situation. Lord I thank you for hearing and for answering my prayers. In Jesus' name, Amen**

4
IDENTITY THEFT

Who are you? What do you see when you look in the mirror? What do people see when they look at you? Do people know the real you or do they know the person you have become to be accepted? How do you behave when you realize people don't accept you for who you really are? Have you reinvented yourself to be accepted because the real you has been rejected? These are a few tough questions you must address with honesty in order to determine whether or not you have been a victim of identity theft by way of rejection.

The enemy fulfills his purpose by using rejection to steal your identity and destroy your self-perception.

When you are no longer able to be the person God created and intended you to be just for the sole purpose of fitting in, you have fallen victim to the enemy's system of identity theft.

There is a story in the Bible that correlates to the message of the enemy using rejection to execute identity theft. Genesis 29:17-35 highlights rejection in a family and the things produced because of rejection. This particular passage talks about the story of Leah, who received rejection from her father and her husband and the rejection she received was solely because of her physical appearance. The first way God defends Leah is by giving her a fruitful womb (vs. 31). Leah had the ability to give birth even in the midst of rejection. However, one must be cautious of what is being reproduced during rejection. Because Leah received so much rejection for most of her life, she found happiness and contentment in the part of her identity associated with giving birth. However, she named each one of her sons according to her state of mind as a result of the rejection. She named her first son Reuben (vs. 32) and his name meant, "The Lord sees." She named her second son Simeon (vs. 33) and his name meant, "The Lord hears." She named her third son Levi (vs. 34) and his name meant "joined." She simply wanted her husband to be joined to her because she bore his sons. Before we get to the name of her fourth son, let's look at what was reproduced during rejection. Leah gave birth to the desire to be seen, to be heard, and to be joined to or fit in. God revealed to me while writing this book that rejection will wear you down mentally and you will lose your identity.

<u>You will then live a life pursuing a mission of being seen, being heard and fitting in!</u>

However, something finally happened after she birthed the fourth son. Leah rediscovered her purpose and no longer allowed the rejection to impact her identity. Leah named her fourth son Judah, (vs. 35), and that name simply means "praise." It was through the son Judah that Leah was vindicated; for Jesus' lineage could be traced back to the tribe of Judah. Leah may have been rejected by man, but she was chosen by God!

Pray this prayer: **Lord I am sorry for thinking you made a mistake in the way you made me. I am sorry for not living to my fullest potential exactly the way you created me to be. Forgive me for valuing man's opinion of me more than your purpose for me. Lord I am sorry for not being confident in the person you destined and designed me to be. I ask that you give me another chance to be the real me. I pray that you allow me the grace to rediscover the person that will** *bring you the greatest joy; because the greatest joy is to fulfill your purpose for my life. Lord I realize you made no mistakes when you created me and I am assured that I am fearfully and wonderfully made. You have equipped me with everything I need to live in my purpose. Lord I thank you for hearing and answering my prayer. In Jesus' name, Amen*

5
Puzzle Pieces: Functional Dysfunction

Have you ever been working on putting a puzzle together and finish the puzzle only to realize one or two pieces were missing? Or during the process you look at one of the pieces and think, "What exactly is this and what part of the picture is this?" When looking at all of the puzzle pieces there's an implication that the pieces will only be acceptable after they are joined together to make the complete picture. The key is to find the appropriate pieces to connect to make the intended picture. Just as it takes all of the pieces of the puzzle to form one beautiful picture, it requires all of the members of the body to form the church that Christ speaks about.

Let's examine what happens in the body of believers when various members of the body have experienced rejection.

First, at some point in our lives we decided we needed a remedy or a solution to the way we were going about doing things; and in turn we decided to give Jesus our heart and allow Him to be our Savior. Keep in mind that the church is comprised of damaged, broken and hurting people who are trying to find a solution and a way to fit in; and, therefore, we are a mass of broken pieces trying to find our rightful place to form a healthy body.

In our best attempts, it is impossible to form a healthy body from broken pieces or broken members. Think about it this way. If each member is already broken, how is it possible to make or create something that is whole that will function appropriately? Remember, we are dealing with many pieces/members to make a beautiful picture/church. However, some of the pieces/members may not be wholly healed from past rejection. When proper healing has not taken place, it then becomes easy to repeat the cycle of rejection. Unfortunately, some people are oblivious to their behavior and how it impacts the body. Some of the members have learned to function in their dysfunction without addressing the elephant in the room.

I study behavior patterns and here is my simple approach to every person I encounter. I approach each person with the mindset of, "The way you do things is reflective of what you consider to be NORMAL in your world." This mindset gives me the liberty of understanding people where they are without making any judgments. From the drug dealer to the pimp, from the prostitute to the drug addict, from the homosexual to the promiscuous heterosexual, from the thief to the murderer, from the lay member in the church to the leader of any great organization; the way people behave, treat people or view situations is normal to them. One person's normal may be another person's abnormal and instead of rejecting them because of the way they do things, I simply try to figure out why they do it and where they learned to do it; getting to the root of the behavior.

With that being said, there's a common phrase that says, *"Hurt people hurt people."* I would like to change that phrase and say, **"Rejected people reject people."** Many people in the church operate from a position of rejection; and this is seen from two different angles of the spectrum of rejection.

One perspective is because people in the church have rejected them, they resolve to doing things just to be accepted, but ultimately never reaching their maximum potential since they are seeking approval from a man or woman, who coincidentally has experienced rejection as well and suppressed it by becoming "over spiritual."

The other identifying trait from the opposite end of the rejection spectrum is the person who has the inability to include others or the inability to see the good in others. Their tendency is to first question people's motives, search for the worst and search for reasons that will confirm their suspicions or apprehensions.

There is a dilemma in the church body, which consists of many members who have not dealt with or overcome rejection; and, as a result, they are continuing the cycle with unsuspecting individuals. It is all a plan in the enemy's systematic approach to steal, kill and destroy. Satan is fine with us being a group of pieces not fully joined and functioning in our dysfunction. He is accomplishing his mission if there is discord and there is no unity and peace. We must seek God for the healing needed to get over the rejection so that it is not reproduced to others.

Pray this prayer: **Lord I thank you for opening my eyes to what I could not initially see. Thank you for giving me clarity where there has been confusion. I ask that you forgive me for giving up on people because they did not fit my mold of normal. I ask that you forgive me for rejecting people because I was rejected and for trying to be accepted as a result of the rejection I encountered. I am now fully aware of the enemy's devices and I want to be healed in every area I've** *experienced rejection. I thank you for hearing and answering my prayer. In Jesus' name, Amen*

PART 3

DEALING WITH REJECTION

6

THE TRUTH, THE WOUND, THE SCAR

In order to deal with rejection, you must be able to admit that it happened and identify the feelings and emotions associated with that experience.

Why is it so hard to admit the pain of what you feel when you have been rejected? Has rejection caused you to form a barrier and close yourself up to possible fruitful relationships? Has it caused you to be someone you are not happy with when you look in the mirror? What is so scary to you that you can't live in the truth of who you really are? Why do you feel comfortable living the way you think others want you to live instead of the way God created you to live?

Keep in mind that all people have experienced some form of rejection, and it is possible to be rejected but still chosen. The good news is God did not consult us in choosing us. As a matter of fact, He already knew we would give Him so many reasons and excuses as to why we are not worthy of being chosen because of our limited understanding of His love and purpose for our lives. The scripture lets us know in John 15:16a:

"Ye have not chosen me, but I have chosen you, and ordained you"

We don't have a choice in whom God chooses, and just like God chose the rejects of Jesus' time, He is still choosing the rejects of our time!

I've seen the impact of rejection in various persons' lives. Rejection will cause a person to feel like a failure, will cause one to settle and will also cause one to live a double lifestyle. I can recall a particular situation where I've seen rejection remove a person from who she really is and who God called her to be. Based on my observations, this person's overt and covert behaviors suggest a lifestyle of denial. **Overt** means: *Opened to view or knowledge; not concealed or secret*. And, **covert** means: *Concealed, secret, disguised or covered*.

This person displays overt behaviors that contradict the truth of who she really is; but her covert behaviors indirectly reveal the character flaws. Trying to cover up the impact of rejection through fabricated social status or through irresponsible extracurricular activities, this person becomes a walking contradiction. What keeps a person from admitting the truth?

FINDING THE YES IN THE NO

As a counselor, one of the most difficult things to do is to help a person who denies the truth of who they are and where they are. It is important to acknowledge the truth, no matter how painful or embarrassing it may be so there can be an avenue to get to the root of the problem and allow healing to begin to occur.

When the truth is not acknowledged, the wound becomes vulnerable to repeated injury. One of the definitions of **wound** is: *An injury or hurt to feelings, sensibilities, reputation, etc.*

Therefore, it can be implied that rejection causes a **wound**. An untreated wound will not heal over time and will create weakness in other areas. It is important to understand that avoidance does not make the issue go away. In addition, suppression of the wound only guarantees a potential eruption after so much pressure and stress is applied to the wound. The wound will give a person access to begin the healing process by simply treating the hurt place. As painful as that place may be, if treated with love, gentleness and wisdom, healing can be activated.

A **scar** is: *A mark left by a healed wound, sore or burn.* The scar serves as a reminder of where the painful spot once was. The scar can also be revered as a permanent souvenir of healing and survival. What scars do you have that serve as a reminder of a place that was once wounded? Your scar should not be used symbolically for pity, but as a memento of survival. And if you survived that painful wounded place, you can thrive in the place of healing and wholeness. Does this process happen overnight? Probably not and that's because the wound did not happen overnight and neither was it addressed overnight. It may be a challenge to get to an authentic place of healing, however, it is attainable because God wants you to be healed and whole.

Pray this prayer: **Lord I pray right now in reference to the overt and covert behavior patterns I have acquired as a result of the rejection. I ask that you forgive me for lying to you, to myself and to everyone around me. I ask that you forgive me for being too afraid to trust you with the honesty of acknowledging my hurt feelings. I ask for your help in my mind, because it is my mind that controls my behaviors. I pray that you give me a strong and a sound mind, even in the face of rejection. Help me not to have the painful memories associated with what I felt. I pray that you go to the wounded place and heal me and make me whole. Help me to see the scar, but understand the scar is proof that I am healed. The scar is the proof of the grace you gave me to survive. I** *need help not only to survive, but also to move to thriving in where you have placed me. I thank you for hearing and for answering my prayer. In Jesus' name, Amen*

7
OUT OF CONTROL

Have you resolved to live in a bubble, to live in what you would consider to be a safe place so that you don't have to deal with rejection? Have you decided you would take control over your life and your environment because rejection caused serious pain in your life? Have you built walls around your heart so no one could get to the place that was once hurt? Is it possible that you have tried to manufacture a safe place and maintain control in every area?

People develop a subset of negative behaviors as a result of being rejected. Consequently, these negative behaviors allow them to be in control and receive the

YES they did not receive initially. It's not a good YES, however it is the YES they accept because they have constructed the situation and the outcome. The YES they receive is a form of comfort because the behaviors have become a choice. Nonetheless, the individuals are out of control because the NO still controls their lives. Here are a few behaviors and scenarios to consider which support this:

VERBAL AGGRESSION

Have you encountered someone who is verbally aggressive in every response and wondered why? It is possible the person was rejected for being nice so the behavior then turned into verbal aggression simply to receive the YES and gain control. The person resorts to verbal aggression to get people to back away but also to control the other person's interaction or approach.

MISTRUST

Why do you have such a problem with trust and refuse to trust anyone? It is possible when you decided to trust, someone hurt you. That hurt was a form of rejection and a way of saying NO. Therefore, you have resorted to mistrust of everyone because it gives you control over the situation. You have control over people hurting you, control over your heart; and that is your YES!

BLAME GAME

Why do you have such a problem with blaming others? It is likely that blaming becomes easy because it places the responsibility of the outcome on someone else rather than on you. Blaming others is your way of having control over the situation. Blaming becomes your safe place and a way you tell yourself YES!

SELF-INDULGENCE/ADDICTION

Why do you self-indulge and make poor choices in an effort to foster happiness with little consideration for your body or your budget? It is probable that you are covering up an instance of rejection through self-indulgence or addictions. Self-indulgence falsifies a sense of love for yourself. Addictions are a coping mechanism used as a temporary fix for a bigger problem, which is rejection. Instead of dealing with the hurt feelings, self-indulgence and addictions become the safe place, a place where you are accepted and a place where you can hear or feel a YES!

LYING

Why do you lie when the truth is evident? It is conceivable that at some point when you told the truth, you were rejected. Telling a lie gave you a false sense of control over the situation. You told yourself YES and decided to never let another person tell you NO. Your lying became your safe place, your place of getting the outcome you want!

PROMISCUITY

Promiscuity occurs for various reasons, but I want to approach this from the viewpoint void of previous sexual violations. It is possible a female has been rejected or hurt and resorts to promiscuity as a way of receiving a YES. It is a dangerous thing when a woman associates her body with receiving a YES simply because she has been told NO in other areas. Promiscuity then becomes a safe place and a way of control all in an attempt to obtain a YES!

There are other behaviors that can be added to this list that can be referenced as a safe place, an avenue of control just to receive a YES. Rejection will produce a subset of negative behaviors if the rejection and the feelings surrounding that rejection are not addressed. One must be open to relive the incident, acknowledge the pain associated with it and then allow healing to occur. Although you may create a situation where you feel you will not give anyone a chance to tell you NO, you are still not healed. God wants you healed and whole. He wants to be your safe place. He wants to be your place of refuge and comfort. The Bible says in Psalm 121: 1,2: *I will lift up mine eyes to the hills from whence cometh my help. My help cometh from the Lord, which made heaven and earth.*

You must be assured that God wants to help you deal with the situation and with the pain associated with the situation. I encourage you to look up to the Creator of this universe, the Creator of heaven and earth. Even if you allowed yourself to get involved in situations you knew were contrary to His will for your life, look up and let Him help you.

Pray This Prayer: **Lord I thank you for opening my eyes and showing me how rejection has produced a subset of negative behaviors in my life. When I am honest with myself and honest with you, I realize I have found myself in one of these areas. I realize I have tried to maintain control over my life and done things to appear as though I am in control. I also acknowledge that I have made a mess with my life trying to control it on my own. Although these behaviors do not please you, in some type of way they made me feel safe. Lord I ask that you forgive me for trying to create a YES by ultimately telling you NO! I ask that you forgive me for trying to control my life and write my own story with a perfect ending. I** *realize there is a greater plan for my life and the greater plan will be revealed as I submit to your perfect will for my life. Father I ask that you erase the pain of the memories associated with the rejection. I ask that you rebuild me, reconstruct me, heal me and make me whole. I understand I cannot do this on my own and there may be times I may make mistakes, but I trust you to get me through this. Thank you for thinking enough of me to allow me to see myself and for giving me a chance to repent. You are the Creator of the universe and there is nothing created that you cannot handle. Lord in the simplest way I know how to say it; my prayer is simply* HELP ME! *I receive your healing today and I receive the best you have for me. Thank you for hearing and for answering my prayer. In Jesus' name, Amen*

8
THE SILENT KILLER

When was the last time you sat in a quiet environment with no music, no television, no one surrounding you and no other outside influences? I do this quite often because silence generates creativity for me, and it also promotes peace. I can ride for hours in silence noticing only the sound of the tires hitting the pavement or the sound of other cars driving by. I can sit in my apartment for hours in silence with no television, no music and no other outside interference. In this instance, silence is welcomed and appreciated. However, there are situations where silence can be viewed as rejection, thus becoming the silent killer.

How do you feel when you ask someone a question knowing the person hears you but still chooses not to respond? Ignoring is a form of silence and also a form of rejection. To ignore someone is to reject them or to refuse to allow the person access into your space if only for a moment. You've seen it over and over again throughout life; sometimes you are on the giving end and sometimes you are on the receiving end.

Consider a child who asks a parent for something and the parent ignores the child purposely or unintentionally. A small child will generally ask until the request is addressed. A teenager may walk away in frustration feeling somewhat defeated in an attempt to gain their parent's attention. What about the child who acts out at school because their parents' busy lives cause the child to be ignored? Or what about the child who adapts extreme behaviors in an attempt to gain attention from anyone who is willing to address them? We witness it more often than not and sometimes these same children fall into the system and become labeled as delinquents or having emotional disorders all because they were ignored. We see the children get involved in gangs as a means of acceptance; they engage in behaviors detrimental to their future because they were given the silent treatment. They are looking for a YES!

Another possible scenario happens in marriages. It is common to see a wife try and have a discussion with her husband while he is watching a sporting event or some other television show. The wife will generally get ignored because the husband's attention is elsewhere. Or perhaps the wife is preoccupied with another task when the husband makes a request and her lack of response makes him feel ignored. These small seeds are planted and sometimes watered by repeated behaviors. Little by little, the enemy creates division in the marriage by starting with small things and then moving on to something bigger. Eventually, the problem becomes bigger than being ignored. Consequently, it becomes difficult to address the problem or get to the root of it because there is a break down in communication. Silence will kill, especially when the appropriate response is to make a sound with your voice.

Pray this prayer: **Lord I thank you once again for opening my eyes to the silent killer. I thank you for showing me how being ignored has caused me to behave differently just to gain attention and acceptance. I also thank you for showing me how I might be guilty of creating this same feeling in someone else through my intentional and unintentional behavior. I ask that you forgive me for the ways in which I have contributed to someone else's downfall. I thank you for the grace** *to see myself and for loving me enough to give me an opportunity to do better. I thank you for hearing and answering my prayer. In Jesus' name, Amen*

9
DEAL WITH IT

Why is it so difficult for us to understand and accept rejection? Have we been made to believe that we are somehow perfect individuals and everyone we come in contact with will accept us? Have we been made to feel as though failure is final, and as a result, we consider rejection as failure? How does rejection resemble failure? Is it possible to learn anything from any situation and make improvements in yourself if the answer is always yes? These are some questions I want you to ponder as you begin to read this section. Let's look at this scripture and try to answer these questions with this scripture. The Bible says in 2 Corinthians 4:17: *"For our light affliction, which is but for a moment, worketh for us a far more exceeding and eternal weight of glory"*

You must understand whatever the situation, it is only for a moment, and if it is rejection in a small moment, it is working in you and working for you something greater than you can understand in that moment. As a matter of fact, it's working something in the eternal realm, so why not endure something in the moment for the possibility of adding to your eternal glory?

Why is it hard to accept it? It is conceivable that our natural minds really can't grasp the concept of eternity or something eternal. We live in a world that operates according to times and seasons and we see things as beginning, in between and ending. We have limited capacity to grasp something not ending, or to understand the existence of something after an ending. Again, we are looking at things from the concept of time, from start to finish or from beginning to an expiration date. We hardly ever consider the concept of eternity, especially not on a day-to-day basis. I submit to you that there are two times in which we consider eternity:

1. **The moment we accept Christ as our Lord and Savior**
2. **The moment someone close to us dies**

Those are the two times eternity is in the forefront of our minds. Therefore, it's difficult to comprehend something we've never seen or experienced and this is the reason rejection can seem final because in our restricted thinking and the way we approach the concept of time, there is usually nothing after NO!

So how should you deal with rejection? First you should acknowledge how it made you feel. Deal with the pain of it and the devastation of the rejection you experienced. You should be able to admit the negative feelings you experienced associated with the rejection. Be honest and assess whether or not you have been able to move forward or how you've become stagnant because the rejection seemed final.

Secondly, God shared with me this simple phrase when dealing with rejection: **You must have assurance in God's allowance.** Rest assured, if God allowed it to happen, then He has something better for you. There can be several factors to Him allowing you to be rejected, but you must be confident in knowing that it is working for your good. The Bible says in Romans 8:28:

"And we know that all things work together for good to them that love God, to them who are the called according to his purpose."

Understand that people have a choice and they can either accept you or reject you. If you are rejected, learn that life does not stop, realize the rejection is working for your good and commit to finding the YES in the NO!

Pray this prayer: **Lord** *I thank you for every situation you have allowed to happen in my life. I also thank you for the strength and commitment to deal with all of the rejection. I give to you my hurt feelings, my damaged emotions, my clouded vision and my broken heart. I ask that you repair me so that I can be even more effective for you. I thank you for hearing and for answering my prayer. In Jesus' name, Amen*

JOURNALING EXERCISE

DEALING WITH REJECTION

Identify at least 5 devastating situations in which you were rejected; be it from childhood or as an adult.

_____
_____
_____
_____
_____

Identify the feelings and thoughts you had in that moment of rejection. Also identify the thoughts and feelings you had days, months or years later because of the devastation. (Referring back to the 5 most devastating situations in which you were rejected)

_____
_____
_____
_____
_____

Identify the negative subset of behaviors that were acquired after experiencing the rejection. (If applicable)

_____
_____
_____
_____
_____

Identify ways in which your life got worse and also identify ways in which your life improved after experiencing the rejection.

_____
_____
_____
_____
_____

Note: If you can think of more than 5 devastating experiences, feel free to write about those as well. But follow this format for addressing each experience.

AFFIRMATION: I willingly accept everything that did not happen, knowing that I can do nothing to change it. I am equipped with everything I need to be successful in every type of relationship I may encounter. I am valuable, I am capable and I am confident in who God created me to be!

PART 4

OVERCOMING REJECTION

10
GET THE ROOT OUT

A tree is identified by the fruit it produces and in order for the fruit to grow on the tree, the roots must be solidified in the ground. If the branches are cut off, a tree can still produce fruit because the roots are still in place. How does this apply to overcoming rejection? There are two particular references in Scripture I want to highlight in order to help with overcoming rejection by getting the root out. The first example is found in Amos 2:9:

"Yet destroyed I the Amorite before them, whose height was like the height of the cedars, and he was strong as the oaks; yet I destroyed his fruit from above, and his roots from beneath."

From this simple scripture God opened my eyes to see what deliverance from any situation looks like. When deliverance takes place, the root is destroyed and the fruit produced from the tree is destroyed. Therefore when true deliverance takes place, you no longer see the fruit of what the person used to be entangled in, the root is destroyed and the fruit can no longer grow.

Well, what happens if you don't destroy the root? Let's look at Job 14:7-9: *"For there is hope of a tree, if it be cut down, that it will sprout again, and the tender branch thereof will not cease. Though the root thereof wax old in the earth, and the stock thereof die in the ground; Yet through the scent of water it will bud, and bring forth boughs like a plant."*

This Scripture is also applicable when trying to understand how to overcome rejection. Just like a tree will bud again if the roots are still in the ground and detect the scent of water, a human will reproduce those behaviors associated with the rejection if the root of rejection is not destroyed. Simply put, when something triggers that old place of rejection, you will see those behaviors associated with the rejection again.

I can recall a situation in which a person was trying to overcome issues of rejection by seeking approval through associations. The behaviors the person was displaying was instability, but the root of the instability was past rejection from childhood through adulthood. To overcome the rejection, the person tried to simply change his environment. Change is good and change of environment is great. However, when you don't deal with the root of the problem, your location may change, but your mind and emotions remain in that same, wounded place and when rejection occurs again, the cycle repeats itself. So instead of running away from the problem or trying to cover it up with associations or any other camouflaged behaviors, get to the root of the rejection. Look within yourself to get beyond the symptoms of rejection and dig deeper to get to the root of it so the cycle does not repeat itself.

I challenge you today to look within yourself and deal honestly with your motives behind doing what you do. If your motives are driven by proving people wrong, you should change them. Your focus should simply be on doing what makes God happy. If you are motivated by hearing "you did a great job", then change your motives because sometimes you may not receive positive feedback. Be confident in your God-given ability, and use that ability to give God glory in the earth. When He wants to acknowledge that gift, He will bring you before great men and women!

Pray this prayer: **Lord I pray right now that you destroy the roots of rejection and desensitize me to the triggers of rejection.** *I realize I have allowed this to take root in my heart and I also realize some situations are painful reminders of how the pain felt. Lord I know I cannot be effective and live out your purpose for my life if I constantly stay in this place of hurt. You are aware of the hurts and the pains I feel and I believe you want to heal me. Lord I ask that you forgive me for holding on to the memories of the past. Forgive me for not forgiving those who have hurt me. I want to reflect you in every way of my life and I don't want things to be signs to others that I have not gotten over situations. Lord I want to walk in freedom and in love. I thank you for hearing and for answering my prayers. In Jesus' name, Amen*

11

FROM "WHY NOT" to "WHAT NOW"

In order to overcome rejection and to gain clarity from certain situations, sometimes you have to ask questions. Therefore, one of the best questions to ask when trying to overcome rejection is "What now?"

The question of "what now" has a subtle suggestion that you are willing to do something different to get a different outcome. It suggests the willingness to move forward beyond the point of rejection with a different focus. We spend so much time asking "why not" because we somehow want a solution or an acceptable answer as to why it did not happen, an answer that will appease us or an answer that will soothe our bruised egos.

When you begin to reflect on the path you have taken to get where you are now, what are some things you don't have that thought you needed? Can you think of a particular situation in which you were told NO and you felt as though your world would crumble? Some disappointments make it hard to comprehend and some setbacks cloud our ability to see the good in things at that moment. Occasionally we can't see the good in it because we think we have just been rejected from what we thought was best for us at that moment!

Pray this prayer: **Lord help me in those times where I felt I was rejected from something good. Help me in those times when I can't see the good in the rejection because I looked at the situation as a good one.**

During those times ease the pain and settle my mind. Cause me to understand that if you did not allow it, then it is not what you wanted for my life. Forgive me for thinking I know better than you and for crying about what you did not allow me to have. Forgive me for lacking maturity and for pouting about situations and people you do not want to have access into my life. Thank you for hearing and for answering my prayer. In Jesus' name, Amen

Let's take a trip down memory lane and reflect on the perfect scenario that ended with a not so perfect ending, simply because we did not write the script. There is a scripture in Hebrews 12:2 that says, **"*Looking unto Jesus the author and finisher of our faith; who for the joy that was set before him endured the cross, despising the shame, and is set down at the right hand of the throne of God.*"**

With this scripture we can understand several things. First we understand that Jesus is writing our story and will complete our story. Secondly, we understand in his personal life that He saw something beyond the cross. He had a glimpse of something greater than the cross, something beyond the shame and the pain he had to endure. He was so focused and committed to his purpose that even what seemed to be the greatest and most embarrassing defeat known to man did not stop him. The rejection he felt in the moment did not stop him. He was able to see beyond current situations and embrace future victories. He was able to experience pain and rejection and still know there was something greater on the horizons.

This is why we have to be assured of God's purpose for our lives, know God in a personal way and be familiar with His voice in our lives. There will be some situations that will be painful and down right humiliating, but we have to be focused on the joy that is set before us; which is the fulfillment of our purpose.

Pray this prayer: **Lord I come to you with my eyes lifted, looking to Jesus as the ultimate example. I thank you for everything you have allowed to happen in my life; as painful as it may have been; as unsure as it may have left me; I'm still confident you have purpose for whatever you allow in my life. I thank you for where I am at this point in my life because I am where you would have me to be. I realize there are times where I got stuck in a situation because I was not able to see beyond the present. Lord I ask that you forgive me for the times I lacked maturity and asked why not; as though that question would change your mind. Thank you for the opportunity to grow and see brand new mercies by saying, "What now?" Give me the** *endurance and the stamina to continue to pursue without giving up or giving in. Thank you for hearing and for answering my prayer. In Jesus' name, Amen*

12

DO SOMETHING DIFFERENT

It takes some people days, months and perhaps years to recover from rejection. It is also very common to see people build their life based off some sort of rejection. But what do you do when you don't have days, months or years to recover from rejection? I would like to submit to you a simple solution: **"DO SOMETHING DIFFERENT!"**

Let's take a quick look at St. John 21:3-6: *"Simon Peter saith unto them, I go a fishing. They say unto him, We also go with thee. They went forth, and entered into a ship immediately: and that night they caught nothing. But when the morning was now come, Jesus stood on the shore: but the disciples knew not that it was Jesus. Then Jesus saith unto them, Children, have ye any meat? They answered him, No. And he said unto them, Cast the net on the right side of the ship, and ye shall find. They cast therefore, and now they were not able to draw it for the multitude of fishes."*

Here's an example of professionals being rejected in their trade. What was the purpose in this instance of rejection? Why were they fishing all night and catching nothing? Jesus used the rejection and their vulnerability to get them to a point where they could hear and recognize him. They felt abandoned so they were vulnerable and they went back to doing what was familiar to them; which was fishing. How easy is it to resort to what's familiar after rejection? How easy is it resort to an old familiar relationship, a traditional pattern of thinking, and a common method of coping, only to do what is familiar and not be successful? There is a common phrase that suggests if you continue to do the same thing and expect different results you are operating in insanity.

I believe Jesus used that moment of rejection to point them to Him. The purpose in this rejection was for them to see Jesus and to hear Jesus. He gave them one simple instruction, **"DO SOMETHING DIFFERENT!"** There is an abundance waiting for you when you do something different. Yes you are a professional, and yes you may have gotten used to doing something one way and that one way has proven successful to you. But, in the moment where that familiar method, traditional pattern of thinking and common method of coping no longer brings you success and you get rejected, **DO SOMETHING DIFFERENT!**

Pray this prayer: **Lord I thank you for opening my eyes to how I may overcome rejection by simply doing something different. I realize I became stuck in a system of thinking, a method of coping and familiar strategies that brought me success in the past. I understand that there needs to be a change in my approach if I want to experience success beyond the rejection. Forgive me for doing things the same way without consulting you and expecting different results. I yield my thinking to you and I pray that you open my eyes so that I may see you and my ears that I may hear you clearly as you give me new strategies to ensure success. Thank you for hearing and answering my prayers. In Jesus' name, Amen**

JOURNALING EXERCISE

OVERCOMING REJECTION

Identify triggers (places, situations, people, etc.) that cause you to be reminded of the devastating impact of the root of rejection.

_____
_____
_____
_____

Identify patterns of behavior or "stinking thinking" you have adapted as a result of the root of rejection.

_____
_____
_____
_____

If past rejection has caused you to become stagnant or develop a fear of rejection, what can you do to move forward and overcome that fear?

_____
_____
_____

Identify the old relationships, familiar coping methods and traditional thinking you resort to when faced with rejection.

What have you learned about yourself from this exercise? What can you do differently that will ensure success in the face of rejection?

AFFIRMATION: I accept the positive as well as the negative with every type of rejection I experienced. I have learned and I will continue to learn from these experiences. I am not a failure because I was rejected. I am still able to succeed.

PART 5

DISCOVERING GOD'S PURPOSE THROUGH REJECTION

13
AN INSIDE JOB

Would you agree that a person's behavior is reflective of his or her inner thoughts, be it positive or negative? Is it safe to conclude that while treating symptoms may bring temporary relief, hopes for permanent change lies in getting to the root of the malfunction? As human beings it is easy to focus on the obvious, external, tangible displays of negative behavior simply because we sometimes lack the patience or the knowledge to work beyond what is on display; however, God in His infinite wisdom and sovereignty knows exactly what to do cultivate what's on the inside of us. He also knows how to do it in private and then let it be a public display for His glory. Let's visit the story in Jeremiah 18:3-6: *Then I went down to the potter's house, and, behold, he wrought a work on the wheels. And the vessel that he made of clay was marred in the hands of the potter: so he made it again another vessel, as seemed good to the potter to make it. Then the word of the Lord came to me saying, 'O house of Israel, cannot I do with you as this potter?' Saith the Lord, 'Behold as the clay is in the potter's hand, so are ye in mine hand, O house of Israel.'*

If we focus on verse 4 and look at it through the lens of rejection, we see the potter:

1. Knows what the end should look like;
2. The potter was not pleased with what he created with his own hands;

3. The potter knew if he put the first piece he created on display it would have been rejected by others because it was not good enough.

The potter rejected the initial vessel because it was not what he intended it to be. The beauty of this story is the fact that it was an **INSIDE JOB** and the image He made did not have a choice. The handcrafted artwork could not jump off the wheel before the potter was finished. It was in a place of total surrender and submission to the hands of the potter. There was a dual purpose to this procedure:

1. He works on the inside of us so we can reflect his outward glory.
2. He works on us in private (inside job) so we can be a public display.

How many times have you felt like you jumped off the wheel before the work was completed in you, only to be rejected by what you were so eager to get to? How many times have you lacked the surrender and submission to God because you simply thought, "Do I have to go through this again?" God already has a picture in mind of what you shall become, and if you don't resemble that picture when He removes you from the wheel, He'll allow you to go through rejection in order for you to become what He sees! The easiest way for you to become what He sees is to simply submit and to surrender.

Pray this prayer: **Lord, I thank You for loving me enough to want me to be a vessel that walks in purpose and as a reflection of your glory. I ask that You forgive me for jumping off the wheel prematurely because I could not submit to You and surrender to the process. I'm sorry for questioning the purpose of going through something again when I was not honest enough with myself to know I didn't pass the test the first** *time. Lord, I thank You for the patience You exercise with me in being willing to put me back on the wheel. Lord, help me to surrender to You and trust Your way of doing things in my life. Thank You for hearing and for answering my prayers. In Jesus' name, Amen*

14
PRESERVED ON PURPOSE

There are certain lengths and extremes people go through to protect something valuable. When there is value in a thing or person, different and sometimes drastic measures are taken to safeguard against destruction. If we feel this way about our things and certain people, imagine how God feels about His creation! God will use rejection to protect you from what could potentially destroy you and preserve you for what will be beneficial to you.

God already had our purpose in mind before He created us. The purpose began before He formed us in our mother's womb just like He told the Prophet

Jeremiah in Jeremiah 1:6: *"Before I formed thee in the belly I knew thee; and before thou camest forth out of the womb I sanctified thee, and I ordained thee a prophet unto the nations."*

Therefore, if God knew us before we even knew ourselves, He already knew what we would become and He knew the process to our becoming. We must try to understand in our limited minds that God sees the end of the things and He knows the rejection in the middle is what we need to appropriately and successfully get to the end of this journey. Remember, the rejection you encounter is only temporary. God knew there was a potential for you to be destroyed, so He allowed the rejection just for your preservation. He allowed the rejection to happen because He was still cultivating the greatness that is within you. God values you! Therefore, if you have to be rejected by what you think is good, realize that God is aware of what is best!

There will be times when you are rejected not because you are not qualified or because you are not good enough, but simply because the people are not ready for everything that comes with you. In those times, remind yourself that if they choose to reject you, then God allowed it because He sees their hearts and knows their minds are not in the right place to handle what He is capable of doing. Subsequently, you have to value yourself enough not to force something and trust in God's sovereignty. You did not lose any value in the rejection; you actually maintained your value because God views what you have as priceless and worthy to be preserved! Remember, there is still a YES in the NO!

Pray this prayer: **Lord,** *I thank You for seeing beyond where I am right now. I thank You for Your wisdom and Your knowledge of every event in my life. I believe You have ordered my steps and predestined this moment of prayer. I thank You that through rejection, You have allowed me to become the person You want. I thank You for keeping me and preserving me for what You created for me. I thank You for preserving it for me and I thank You for preserving me for it. In spite of the painful process I may have endured, the end of the process is worth the pain. Lord, I pray that You keep my heart and my mind in a posture of gratitude to appreciate what You have preserved for me. I thank You for hearing and for answering my prayer. In Jesus' name, Amen*

15
IT'S ALL ABOUT YOU

What is purpose? As defined by Dictionary.com, **purpose** is *the reason for which something exists or is done, made, used, etc.; an intended or desired result; end; aim; goal.*

Do you know the reason for which you exist? The purpose for which you lived is most likely how you will be remembered in the minds and hearts of the people you were closely connected to. But the question still remains: do you know your purpose? If the answer is yes, then it should be easy to accept the paths you must travel in order to fulfill your purpose, right? WRONG!

As human beings, we are likely to choose the path of least resistance; the path with fewer obstacles, hurdles, detours and damaged roads. We are in such a "fast-paced, on demand, time is of the essence" society until we try to choose the easiest route to get to the desired goal. The purpose of GPS is to pinpoint the quickest route to get to your final destination. One use of the Internet contains the ability to rapidly access information with the clicking of a mouse or tapping of the finger. Why would you make it hard on yourself when it is made easy for you? We value our time so we try to do as much "stuff" that can be done with as little time consumption as possible.

This brings me to two questions: Why would there be purpose in rejection and how can you find God's purpose for the occurrence? Since He's an omniscient, omnipresent, omnipotent and sovereign God, shouldn't He create a smooth path for your purpose? Shouldn't He already know where there may be a roadblock and prepare you for an alternative route instead of allowing you to experience the rejection of a "DETOUR" or "ROAD CLOSED" sign?

I feel there is purpose in rejection because it causes you to:

1. Re-evalute;
2. Humble yourself;
3. Seek for guidance;
4. Submit to the will of God and His direction.

All of these things- **re-evaluating, humbling, seeking and submitting**- will ultimately strengthen you and help you to develop stronger muscles in God. You have to remember that God sees your end from your beginning. Many people may speak into your life concerning certain destinations along your process of becoming, but God sees and knows your end. Sometimes the rejection happens because you may arrive at the destination too soon. You may not be ready for what is at the end and the end may not be complete for you.

The rejection will cause you to **re-evaluate** yourself and the motives behind your desires for wanting to receive something or to have access to something. You will also re-evaluate your commitment to what you are pursuing: is it worth it or should you try something else?

The rejection will cause you **to humble** yourself. It will initiate a sense of helplessness and a desire to receive help. It will definitely let you know that you are NOT the final authority and you can't control every outcome. It will cause you to look within yourself. It points the finger at you and you bear the responsibility of hopefully making necessary changes.

FINDING THE YES IN THE NO

The rejection will cause you **to seek** God for an answer. You will begin to seek God for clarity as far as timing and direction. Is this something you should continue to pursue? Is this something you should put on hold? Is it something that you should walk away from? You will have to seek God because you no longer know the answer. Sometimes the rejection is actually a tool God uses to get you back in fellowship with Him.

The rejection will cause you **to submit** your plans and outcomes to God. He has a way of breaking your will, and sometimes your will can be strong and out of line with His will. You have to get to a point of submission, and oftentimes submission does not happen when everything is going your way. Submission usually happens when things get difficult, when nothing seems to be going right and after you have been rejected.

I believe God's ultimate purpose for rejection within each individual is to get that individual totally dependent on Him. He wants you in communion with Him. He desires for you to live a life of submission by trusting Him with your plans and seeking Him for clarity and direction. Ultimately, He wants you to bring Him glory!

My prayer: **Father, I pray now for every person who has read this book. I pray that their understanding has been opened to Your purpose for rejection. I pray when they encounter it again, they will have the knowledge and the power to deal with it accordingly. I pray each person understands there is ultimately a YES even in the NO! I pray for the person who read this book and found themselves crying because they could identify with different scenarios. I pray You heal the wounds and dry the tears. Heal** *every broken heart and wounded spirit that formulated as a result of rejection. I pray specifically for the person who is losing sleep because they are trying to figure out why they did not seem good enough. I come against every addiction that was formed as a result of being rejected. I pray that You redeem the time lost for those who have been stuck in the past because of rejection. I ask that You help each person walk successfully who reads this book. Give clarity where there is confusion; give peace where there is strife and contention; give joy where there is sadness, but most of all let your glory be seen in this and through this. I thank You in advance for the victory in every believer's life. It is in Jesus' name I pray, Amen.*

ACKNOWLEDGMENTS

With an appreciative heart, I express gratitude to those who made it possible for me to write about my experiences and share the revelation God gave to me regarding rejection. I would like to thank:

- My husband, Alex Caldwell, for being the epitome of a provider during this move to Allen, Texas. Because of your understanding and willingness to allow me to be a stay at home mom for a season, I was able to write this book with no pressures, demands or distractions from an employer. Thank you for affording me the opportunity for rest and writing.

- Jasmine and Amber for being loving, understanding and supportive of your Mom during this transitional period. Thank you for being the gifts you are to me with an uncanny ability to understand my verbal and nonverbal communication and ensuring that we always live in a peaceful environment full of love, laughs and fun.

- Paul & Lou Edna Son, for being supportive parents throughout the years. Simply put-- because of you, I am and I can! R.I.P. Dad 06-17-14
- My siblings, Byron Son & Tammy Son, for encouraging me and being two of my biggest encouragers and supporters all of my life.
- The Caldwell family: Billy & Lena, Cassandra, Franklin & DaShune, Tonya, Billy & LaShonda, for taking me in and loving me as your own.
- My Pastor, Avery Wiles & Lady Krystal Wiles and the entire Grace Community Church North Dallas congregation, for your prayers and support of me during this time and this assignment.
- My teacher, my mentor, my counselor, my motivation, Ms. Kathy Charley! Thank you for believing in me and encouraging me to embrace the down time during the shift from Louisiana to Texas. Thank you for giving me the opportunity to teach along side you and equip others to become Certified Christian Counselors. Thank you for your words of wisdom and acts of kindness towards me.

- My editor, Shani Lasana, for your good eye and your sharp mind. I'm simply amazed and speechless with your work and your knowledge, but even more so at how our paths crossed years ago and years later we are together again.
- Adrian Bostick, my graphic designer, for your ability to take my words and bring them to life immediately.
- Dr. Shelita Edwards-McGowan, for your belief in me and being a dear friend.
- To all of my friends who encouraged me, prayed for me, stood with me and held me accountable as I started and completed this journey of writing this book. There's a huge place in my heart for all of you. Thank you.
- Most importantly, to my Lord, the author and finisher of my faith. Thank you seems to be inadequate to accurately depict the gratitude that flows from my heart when I consider everything you have done, are doing and will do in my life. I appreciate you for trusting me enough to open my eyes and giving me the ability to put words to

FINDING THE YES IN THE NO

things that will help heal those who have been hurt by experiencing rejection.

PAULA SON-CALDWELL

www.ingramcontent.com/pod-product-compliance
Lightning Source LLC
LaVergne TN
LVHW041630070426
835507LV00008B/537